Animals

An Alphabet Of 26 Beautiful Bold Beasties

Jennifer Farley

For Jason, Otto & Knuckles

"Animals are such agreeable friends - they ask no questions, they pass no criticisms"
George Elliot

Book design by Jennifer Farley (www.JenFarley.com)

ISBN 978-0-9572837-7-0 (paperback)

First paperback edition May 2021

Published by ooh lovely. (www.oohlovely.com)

Aa

ALLIGATOR

Bb

BEAR

Cc

CAMEL

Dd

DONKEY

Ee

ELEPHANT

Ff

FLAMINGO

Gg

GIRAFFE

Hh

HIPPOPOTAMUS

Ii

INCHWORM

Jj

JAGUAR

Kk

KOALA

LI

LION

Mm

MONKEY

Nn

NARWHAL

Oo

OSTRICH

Pp

PENGUIN

Qq

QUAIL

Rr

ROOSTER

Ss

SNAKE

Tt

TIGER

Uu

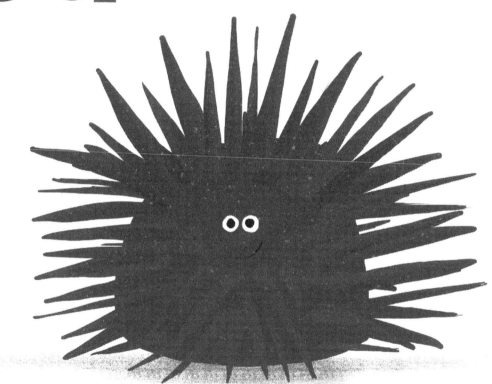

URCHIN

Vv

VULTURE

Ww

WALRUS

Xx

X-RAY FISH

Yy

YAK

Zz

ZEBRA

Aa

Alligators have been living on Earth for millions of years. They are reptiles and sometimes known as 'living fossils'.

Bb

Brown bears or "Grizzly Bears" sleep fo the whole winter. They like to eat seed berries, grasses, deer, elk, fish and inse

Ee

Elephants are the largest animals on land. When they swim in deep water they use their trunk as a snorkel to breathe.

Ff

A flock of flamingos is sometimes known a flamboyance of flamingos. Flamingos ca grow up to 5 feet tall.

Cc Camels store food in their humps. Dromedary camels have one hump, and Bactrian camels have two humps.

Dd A male donkey is called a Jack and a female donkey is called a Jenny or Jennet. Donkeys are gentle and placid animals.

Gg Giraffes are the tallest mammals in the world. They spend most of their lives standing up - even when they sleep.

Hh The name hippopotamus means "river horse" often shortened to hippo. They spend most of their time in water - rivers, lakes and swamps.

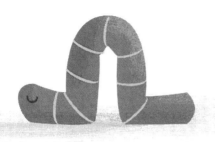

Ii Inchworms get their names because it looks like they are measuring the ground, one inch at a time.

Jj Jaguars are large cats identified by the yellow-orange coats and dark spots. Ea spot looks like a rose and is called a ros

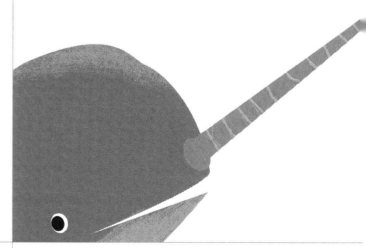

Mm There are over 200 different types of Monkey. The smallest grow to 6 inches while the largest grow up to 3 feet high.

Nn Narwhals are often called the unicorns o the sea. The long tusk protruding from th head is actually a giant tooth.

Kk A baby koala is called a joey. Koala joeys live in their mother's pouch for around six months after they are born.

Ll The lion's mane helps the lion appear bigger and scarier to other animals. The darker the mane, the older the lion.

Oo Ostrich are the largest living bird in the world. They can't fly, but can run fast, hitting speeds of up to 40 miles per hour.

Pp Penguins don't fly. They spend about three quarters of their time in the water, where they are fast swimmers.

Qq The quail is a small bird that inhabits woodland and forest areas around the world. They lay tiny, brightly coloured eggs.

Rr A rooster is a male adult chicken. He tells the flock of female chickens that he's found food with a "took, took, took."

Uu The red sea urchin has the longest lifespan on Earth. It can survive up to 200 years in the wild.

Vv Vultures can stay in the air for hours. Using their long broad wings, they soar gracefully on the warm winds.

Ss There are more than 3,000 species of snakes in the world. The largest snake, the reticulated python, can grow to 30 feet.

Tt Tigers are the largest wild cats in the world. Unlike most members of the cat family, tigers like water and are good swimmers.

Ww Walrus tusks are actually large teeth. They use them to pull themselves out of the water.

Xx X-Ray fish are tiny fish which live in rivers in South America. Their bodies are almost completely see-through.

Yy The Yak's body is covered with a thick, wooly coat. The fur keeps the yak warm in very cold temperatures high in the mountains.

Zz The zebra has the most distinctive coat the animal world. Each Zebra's stripes a unique – no two are exactly alike.

Printed in Great Britain
by Amazon